# TEACH MY DOG TO DO THAT

# TEACH MY DOG TO DO THAT

**Simple tricks for your four-legged friend**

**Jo-Rosie Haffenden
and Nando Brown**

BΦXTREE

First published 2017 by Boxtree
an imprint of Pan Macmillan
20 New Wharf Road, London N1 9RR
Associated companies throughout the world
www.panmacmillan.com

ISBN 978-0-7522-6644-2

1 3 5 7 9 8 6 4 2

A CIP catalogue record for this book is available from the British Library.

Typeset by seagulls.net
Printed and bound by CPI Group (UK) Ltd, Croydon, CR0 4YY

Visit **www.panmacmillan.com** to read more about all our books
and to buy them. You will also find features, author interviews and
news of any author events, and you can sign up for e-newsletters
so that you're always first to hear about our new releases.

# Contents

# Foreword
## by Alexander Armstrong

I never quite know what answer to give when I'm asked
if I'm a 'cat' or 'dog' person because the truth is I'm very
much both. I've lived with cats *and* dogs for as long as I can
remember but I expect very different behaviours from each.
If I went for a long walk and the cat was tailing me all the
way, I think I'd find it a bit unsettling. Equally, if every time
I read the paper on the kitchen table the dog kept walking
up and down the page, trying to rub itself against my face,
I suspect I'd see that in a less-than-endearing light. We
condition our expectations of animal behaviour according
to what we know but – as this excellent book demonstrates
– perhaps we are underestimating our pets by setting the bar
so low. Animals, as we have known for centuries, are capable
of acquiring truly breathtaking skills. This may be sheepdogs
performing feats of herding to simple verbal commands
or the fabulous Pudsey wowing us, and the *BGT* judges,
with his dexterity. But it wasn't until I'd seen Jo-Rosie and
Nando train a chicken to perform a challenging piece of
choreography and a rook to tidy up a room and put all
the mess into a basket that I realized quite how much can
be achieved. There is a whole world of fun to be had with
our pets; a world we can access through simple training
techniques that we, and they, can pick up in no time.

The first dog we had when I was little was a beautiful
yellow lab called Docchan, who'd been bred and trained on

a farm about five miles up the valley from our house in rural Northumberland. But the problem was we discovered that he'd formed such a strong bond with Henry, his trainer, that he was always a bit miserable being away from him. Every few months he'd disappear and, sure enough, we'd eventually get the call from Henry to say he was with him. After a while we admitted defeat and gave him to Henry (who was as devoted to Docchan as Docchan was to him – there's a screenplay in here somewhere, surely) but the whole episode taught me two things. The first was what a phenomenal brain that dog had; time and again he would find his way back to a farm five miles away from us using nothing but a kind of internal canine satnav. The second thing made me promise myself that I would never get someone else to train an animal for me if I could do it myself, because I learnt then that the connection you make with an animal through training is something awe-inspiring and truly special. Instead of merely enjoying the company of the animal you love, you are taking your relationship to a completely new level and forging a deep bond of understanding that turns owning a pet into a two-way partnership that brings huge pleasure and fulfillment to both of you.

Set yourself small but achievable goals with your dog and you'll be amazed at how quickly you progress. And remember at all times: if a chicken can dance, a dog can do ANYTHING. Have fun and good luck!

# Introduction

If you've bought this book for yourself, or had it bought for you as a gift, the chances are you own a dog. Let's face it, it would be an odd book to get if you didn't! So you'll know how close the bond can be between a dog and its family.

We spend huge amounts of time and money on feeding and walking our best friends but training, whether for obedience or for tricks, is often seen as an optional extra. However, we're here to say that the process of trick training can open up a whole new relationship with your dog, whatever their age or breed. If you follow the simple

steps contained in this book, you'll end up with a more stimulated, happier dog and a deeper and more fulfilling relationship with them.

With our busy lives, it's more and more often the case that our dogs spend part of the day alone. In this context it's even more important that we take the time to stimulate our dogs when we are with them. They may have a favourite toy, but imagine if you had only one thing you did for recreation; you'd either quickly become bored of it or it could turn into an unhealthy obsession.

Tracking and chasing down quarry is such a big part of their evolutionary history that coming up with fun ways of recreating some of these behaviours can have massive benefits to your dog's wellbeing and happiness.

Just a few simple changes can quickly build a training vocabulary where the only limit is your imagination.

We can't wait for you to get started.

*Jo-Rosie and Nando*

# The History of Dogs

**T**he domestic dog is the most diverse domesticated species on Earth. So how did this happen? Well, about 10,000 years ago, during the Mesolithic era, man began to settle in camps. As a side product of staying in one place, we started to leave waste on the outskirts of our villages. This waste lured an ancient type of wolf to creep towards the settlements under the cover of darkness and scavenge off the remains from our daily lives. Over time this split the wolves into two distinct lines: the more reserved, who stayed wary of man and would keep their distance, and the wolves who were brave enough to risk proximity to humans. This latter group started to reap the rewards of gaining food without having to expend lots of energy hunting. So, when we arrogantly claim that man domesticated the dog, well, actually it's become evident through looking at remains and blood samples of canines that the dog domesticated itself!

As wolves realized the benefits of hanging around humans, their suspicions decreased over generations and this had another effect. Whenever there is a change in an animal's temperament we know that affects the way the animal looks. Over many generations these wolves slowly started to behave and look different. We started to reward the wolves for acting as lookouts whenever they vocalized at anything unusual in the night, which would alert us to an approaching enemy.

Slowly through the years we would start to breed certain dogs because of their abilities. If one dog was particularly fast, we would choose an equally impressive bitch to increase the likelihood of having a litter of puppies with a similar skill set. Unbeknown to us at the time, we were selectively breeding to emphasize part of what we now call the **predatory action sequence** – which part of that sequence would depend on what we wanted from the dogs. Some jobs needed a keen sense of smell and the ability to track

prey; others needed a dog that could outrun prey we would have trouble catching, and some dogs were needed to bring down large game in groups that otherwise man would injure himself attempting to kill. As a result of breeding specifically emphasized characteristics, we have ended up with dogs that look the same, too. And now, finally, we have *HUNDREDS* of different breeds to choose from. Take a look at your dog now. No, really check them out. Do you know what they were originally bred for, what mix of thousands of years of breeding make up your furry friend? Because in their DNA is the code of a specialist. They may have one or a few of these super powers: scent skills, speed for the chase, bite to grab or to kill or the ability to guard. Now, all dogs have these skills but, depending on the type or breed of dog, they will be better equipped to use them.

Bloodhounds are the king of the nose and will excel in searching for their toys. Collies and pointers give us beautiful examples of eye and stalk, so teaching them to herd a gym ball or stalk a tennis ball is great fun for them. Lurchers love to chase, so using this as a reward will make teaching any behaviour easier. Bull breeds are exceptional grab-biters and love to play tug, which means they'll love the 'Open the Door' trick later. Terriers have the ability to kill prey with a snap of the neck, while gun dogs and guard dogs are driven to possess, which gives us the foundation for our retrieve tricks. And, finally, nobody can quite top the Labrador for their love of food! All jokes aside, this is an important topic if we want to reward dogs in training. And that is where all training begins: rewarding what we like in the hope that we see it more often. It doesn't have to be food but it does have to be fun for your dog.

# Top 5 Dog Rules

## 1. I need regular exercise.

Dogs have a purpose that they have been selectively bred for. Many of those jobs require dogs to be fit, but with that fitness comes a price. Some sled dogs run races of over 1,000 miles and it's claimed that a working Border collie will travel around seventy-five miles every day. Now, we're not suggesting you have to run a marathon with your dog every day but you do need to bear these stats in mind. When researching which breed of dog to get, ensure you have the genuine time – wind, rain or shine – to take your dog for adequate physical exercise. If you use your imagination this doesn't need to be laps of the dog park but instead can mean planned hikes to places of beauty, riding bikes across the downs or exploring the villages of Britain with your best friend in tow.

## 2. I need to go to school too.

Imagine that each day you wake up, go to the gym and then spend the day at home. For a rare few of you that may seem like the ideal lifestyle, but if you are anything like us it sounds like a nightmare. We love physical exercise and we walk every day as well as, on occasion, visit a gym. If this was all we did, though, we know we would be bored out of our minds. As cerebral and social beings we require interaction and to be busy. We want to have goals and challenges as these

things keep us happy. Your dog needs these things, too, be it hiding toys or food for him to find, going to sports classes each week or clicker-training your dog new tricks, as in this book. Put away your phone and interact! It's not only

7

good for your relationship; it's also vital if you want to see your best friend thrive. Education is key; you wouldn't have children without educating them, so remember that teaching dogs new skills isn't a luxury, it's a necessity.

## 3. I need a way to tell you when I've had enough.

Sadly we see dogs all the time that, through no fault of their own, end up having to use visual and audible warnings to tell people they've had enough. Sometimes dogs are in a position where they end up growling, barking or lunging because their subtle attempts to escape just haven't been heard. Make sure your dog has their very own 'fire escape' if a situation is too much. It might be a covered crate where they are always left undisturbed; or their own warm snuggly doggy den in the outhouse; or maybe it's a simple space behind the sofa. Just be sure your dog always has the option to leave a situation instead of having to make himself heard and, as counter-intuitive as it might seem, never punish a dog for growling. It's the equivalent of taking the batteries out of your smoke alarm. If they stop growling you might not be warned of a bite.

## 4. Remember that if it looks like a toy, and smells like a toy – it's just a toy.

Some dogs, and especially puppies, will almost definitely need to chew, but for all dogs this behaviour feels good. The act of chewing releases endorphins and so makes dogs happy. They need things to gnaw on and there are some fabulous options for them on the market. However, if your dog usually steals shoes and you give him an old shoe to chew, remember that he won't be able to tell the difference when a shoe is left by the shoe rack. Equally, squeaky, fluffy and rubbery toys that belong to your kids are fair game unless you store them away at the end of each play session.

## 5. I am what I eat.

Dog foods come in all shapes and sizes these days but some act like rocket fuel for dogs. If your dog food is full of colourful kibble then, as a general rule, it's likely to be on the fast-food scale of dog food. While we're on the subject of food, bin the bowl! A dog's dinner can be the highlight of their day, but eating it from a bowl is excruciatingly boring if you're a born scavenger or hunter. Try scatter feeding or buying food-dispensing toys that will not only slow down your dog's eating, which can be healthier for them, but will also be a good way to mentally stimulate your dog, making them happier.

# Setting Your Dog Up for Success

# Setting Your Dog Up for Success

**I**magine, if you will, that we were teaching you how to use your new mobile phone. If you learnt this skill on the sofa in your front room, then chances are you'd have no problem using your phone in the kitchen, bedroom or even the garden.

There are two things to think about when it comes to teaching our dogs.

1.  Our understanding of the canine learning process so far indicates that dogs aren't very good at generalizing. Let's pretend for a moment that dogs can use mobile phones. If you taught your dog how to use the phone in the kitchen, they don't have the same level of ability to transfer this skill to other rooms as easily as a human does. So, teaching something as simple as a 'sit' should be taught in one place and then practised in many different locations to help make the behaviour more reliable.
2.  Where you choose to teach the behaviour will also have an enormous impact on how quickly and how dependable that behaviour becomes. If we again use the analogy of you learning to get to grips with your new phone, then being taught in the front room where you are feeling secure and comfortable will be much easier than if you were trying to learn the same skill during a rollercoaster ride. Don't forget that dogs see with their

nose, so teaching them at home in a quiet room with minimal distractions is going to give you much more success than if you start your training outside in the park where they will experience a rollercoaster of different scents, sights and sounds to distract them. Ultimately we want them to be able to practise their tricks anywhere, so teach them at home and practise in as many varied places as possible.

# The
# Fundamentals

**T**o train any animal, there are two essential elements: 1) they must understand what you want them to do and know when they've done it and 2) they must want to do it through associating it with rewards. The way we do this with dogs is through **positive reinforcement**.

Positive reinforcement is a term that trainers use to explain part of a technique called **operant conditioning**. We are going to be using this technique but it's nowhere near as complicated as it sounds. What we strive to do in all our training is to set the animal up for success. If the dog isn't grasping the concept quickly, a good trainer will stop, re-evaluate their training plan and work out a clearer way forward for achieving their goal.

Now that you've decided to teach your dog some skills, you are the trainer but don't worry – the days of confrontation and intimidation in animal training are long gone! And buried between the covers of this book are some of the best training plans handwritten by us for you. But before we can jump straight into our new hobby we need to iron out some of the basic concepts. You'll see the terms **mark and reward** repeatedly used throughout the course of this book, so let's break that down.

## Marker

A marker is a way of pinpointing the exact moment Fido does something right. In the show you would have seen us using a clicker; this is an audible marker that allows us to let the dog know the exact moment he did something right. The clicker is a precision tool used to teach a dog new things. Once

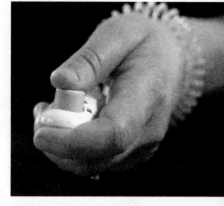

the dog understands what we want and can do it when we ask, you don't need it anymore. It's a useful training tool but you won't need one for the rest of your dog's life, unless of course you're teaching them new things all the time, in which case your dog is one very lucky boy!

Wait! You don't have a clicker with you? No worries, we can use all sorts of things to mark behaviour and dogs are capable of understanding more than one marker, as long as we are consistent. Even as professional animal trainers we can be found without a clicker, so we often train our own dogs using a verbal marker. We use the word 'yes', but any short sharp word said in a happy tone can be used as an effective marker word. Pick one word, but 'good boy' or 'good girl' won't cut it here as we use this type of praise all the time. If you're anything like us we constantly tell our dogs how good they are just for being beautiful, so the marker has to have more meaning behind it. 'Good dog' is just too long to be practical when training, as dogs are fast and can usually perform several behaviours before we finish saying it in our silly, high-pitched, camp voice. If your dog is deaf or hard of hearing then using an audible marker isn't

going to work; for
these dogs you can use
a flicker of a torch or
even a hand signal to
let them know they've
met the criteria to
earn a reward. In other
words, when we talk
about marking (**mark**

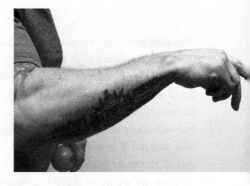

**and reward**), you can use any of the above but it needs to
clearly and distinctively signal to your dog that a reward is
imminent.

Here's a quick exercise you can practise to make sure
you're ready to get this right.

1. Put your dog in another room and have two pots in front
   of you – one full of treats and one empty.
2. Turn on your favourite TV programme.
3. Every time one of the actors blinks you're going to mark
   the behaviour and then move one of the treats from the
   full pot to the empty one.

This may seem like an unnecessary task but it will prevent you from fumbling with your marker and confusing your dog. This quick exercise also teaches you to have an eye for detail and builds your mechanical skills of moving treat to mouth. If you nail this one then once you get your dog out you will easily convince him into thinking that you are a fully fledged dog-training ninja and, trust me, he will love you all the more for it!

Now we are up to speed with our markers we need to work out how to reward the dog. Notice that we don't refer to 'click and treat' in this book and instead use 'mark and reward'. That is because the marker isn't always a clicker and the reward is not always a treat.

We don't decide what the dog finds rewarding (sadly) – they do that. If your dog loves ham then that will be his reward; if he loves tug then that will be his reward; if it's all about that tennis ball being launched – that will do the trick here.

If you are using food then the phrase 'little and often' applies here. The treats only need to be small – around a quarter of the size of your thumbnail is a standard for most medium-sized dogs – but don't be tight! Pay often: the number of treats your dog gets in a session is directly

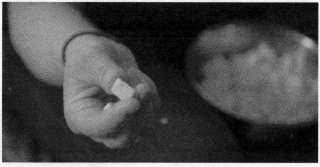

**19**

correlated to how successful your training is and how much of a dude your dog thinks you are. Think of this as doggy currency – we need to pay our dogs for working for us, except we get to pay them with food!

There are many pros to using food in training:

- It allows you to have a high number of repetitions in a session.
- It has the added benefit of building a positive emotional association with you – that means working with your dog and food will make him love you more.

You do need to be careful with your dog's weight, however; there are too many fat dogs waddling around already, so be sure to use healthy treats and to reduce your dog's daily food allowance accordingly.

Some dogs just aren't turned on by food and, if this is the case, it's your job now that you are a dog trainer in the making to find out what it is that can motivate your dog. The first step is to think back to that predatory action sequence and figure out if your dog has a particular trait that we can capitalize on. Try fetch, tug games, searches and lashings of verbal praise as well as cuddles, if your dog likes them!

If we use play as our reward it will generally slow down our training, but we can also get more bang for our buck, so if you're lucky enough to have a dog who loves food *and* toys, I would recommend starting out with food but then switching to toys to put some *oomph* into the behaviour as you start to perfect the exercises.

We do have to consider what dog trainers call the **hierarchy of rewards**. This looks at every individual dog's preferences. For instance, if I were to ask you to rate in order of preference: travelling, museum visits, picnics in the woods, cash or fast cars, the order might be very different between you and your closest friend. Same goes for our dogs. If we put up a list of cheese, hotdogs, frisbee, tug and sniffing other dogs' bottoms, then each of my own dogs will have a very different list. A good trainer knows each dog will have its own likes and dislikes and it's not always a fixed list. If you like chocolate cake it can be the last thing on your mind if you've spent the entire Sunday gorging on Grandma's roast dinner with all the trimmings! And there is only so much cheese a dog can eat – well, unless it's a Labrador, of course! With this in mind it might be a good exercise, before we begin, to write down all the things your dog likes. Then put them into three categories: low, medium and high value. See the one we did for one of our dogs, Fizz the Malinois, before:

- High – Frisbee, chasing a flirt pole, playing tug.
- Medium – Chicken, liver cake, chasing a tennis ball.
- Low – dry dog food, off-lead greetings with other dogs.

What does your dog like?

# It's Supposed to be Fun!

**T**he one golden rule you must not forget when it comes to trick training is that not all tricks are suitable for all dogs, so make sure your dog is happy and healthy.

**Happy** – as far as your dog is concerned, it should be difficult for him to decipher the difference between play and training. The goal is that both of you walk away from your training sessions having had loads of fun as well as

having learnt some new skills. Try to keep your teaching sessions to short fun bursts. Five minutes is a great ballpark figure to aim for, but if you think your dog is losing interest or getting bored, then we need to think about a few different things. Ask yourself the following questions:

**Am I sucking all of the fun out of it?** If you're taking it all too seriously and not enjoying the process, then chances are your pup will have figured this out. If you're not in the mood to train because you've had a rubbish day at work, then skip the training session for the day.

**Am I loving the training so much that I'm being greedy?** One of the enormous benefits to clicker training is that it's so mentally stimulating for dogs that short sessions can exhaust many dogs quicker than taking them out for a walk, but being asked to solve a maths equation when you're already tired can be frustrating and even make you a little resentful about the whole thing. Ensure you don't ask for too much and give your dog a break every now and then to process any lessons learnt.

**Am I paying enough?** All animals (including humans) have one common goal and that is to make the good times start! We also all, however, have a price. If we ask you to help us build our house for free you might tell us, and rightly so, to naff off! If we offer you £200 a day, would you be interested? What about if we upped it to £600 per day? If your dog doesn't look enthused by the idea of training then check you're not being overly tight with the treats. Building a bungalow requires less effort than the attention to detail required to build Buckingham Palace, so the harder the trick, the more you need to pay him.

**Is the particular step you're working on too hard?** Some of the tricks we are going to teach need a certain amount of pre-training of **foundation behaviours**. For instance, the **Open the Door** trick presumes your dog already knows how to **Pull**. Investing time in the more basic training positions is rarely wasted and makes tricks look a lot slicker and advanced training easier.

**Healthy** – this is really important: your dog will need to be relatively fit. Elbow and hip dysplasia is unfortunately very common in many of today's dogs. Any tricks that include any high-impact exercises like jumps would be unsuitable for a dog that suffers with these kinds of issues. Also, consider your dog's physical body – it would probably be unfair to teach a Dachshund to beg with the long back they have. If you are at all unsure of what may or may not be suitable, then try contacting a certified FFTT (Force Free Trick Trainer) Instructor. These guys specialize in teaching tricks and will be able to point you in the right direction.

There is one last thing we need to consider before we start teaching our dogs to become trick dog experts and that is to ensure we set up the environment to help them learn. Prepare your treats, pick up all the excess dog toys, put the other dogs in another room with something like a stuffed kong to keep them occupied, and make sure there is water available for your dog to refresh himself in the breaks.

Our main job is to teach dog trainers and this is probably the single most common mistake we see novice trainers do. Failing to prepare is preparing to fail!

Right then. We're finally ready to start teaching some tricks!

# Foundations

**T**o make sure this process runs as smoothly as possible for both the dog and you, there are some key skills you're both going to need to get to grips with first. Spend time getting these solid and the more complex tricks will be loads easier than you expected.

### Follow a Lure

I know what you're thinking: following food isn't going to be hard for my dog, and you're right, it won't be. The skill, however, lies at the human end of the lead for this part. Get this right now and you'll be teaching much more advanced tricks super simply!

Take out a treat and slowly move the dog around a chair in a circle. The goal is to find the perfect distance where he can follow the lure without snapping at the food or losing interest. Once they are moving around the chair nicely, try luring the dog up onto the chair. First do this standing on the right of the dog, then the left, then in front. This game is a lot more about your handling skills than the dog's brain but it will most certainly help you when teaching other foundations.

# Touch

*Time to train:* 2 weeks at 1 x session per day
*Type of trick:* Useful
*Application:* Can be used for things as simple as moving your
dog off the couch without shouting or as complicated as
voluntary veterinary procedures
*What you will need:* Your hand, a Post-it note and some
tasty treats!

The touch is a **foundation behaviour** that has numerous
different applications and it will be an integral part of so
many of the more-advanced tricks. Like many of these
foundations, it really is worth investing the time to get the
behaviour solid before attempting harder exercises.

1.  The first part of this trick starts with teaching your dog
    how to target a Post-it note. To start you will need to
    stick said Post-it note on the palm of your flat hand and
    then produce your hand to the side of your dog's face –
    close enough so
    the dog wants
    to investigate
    but not so close
    that they try to
    move away from
    it. As soon as
    your dog gives
    it a sniff, mark
    and reward.

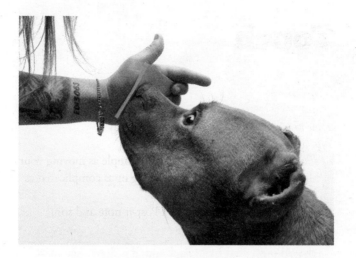

2. Repeat the above but this time, to earn the reward, your dog must actually make contact with the nose to the note. You are looking to achieve ten clean repetitions of this step before moving up to Step 3, as the dog needs to fully understand what he has to do before we move forward with the training. Training dogs is all about repeating things, so buckle up and learn to be patient – it'll be worth it when you start smashing through the tricks later on in the book.

3. This time you can tilt your hand so that your palm faces the floor but the note is hanging down facing your dog. You should be removing the note each time he gets it right, when he gets his reward, and then re-presenting it. If the dog touches the note with enough pressure to move it, click and treat.

4. Next place the Post-it note so that it sits flat against your palm. Present the Post-it on your palm to your dog at the side of his face again but this time a little further away. Wait for the dog to touch. The pressure of his touch

should push your hand back and, if it does, then mark and reward.

5. Now our dog is happily touching the Post-it note and putting pressure on it, it's time to start moving the note from your hand to different surfaces. Remember we've taught them to push, so don't put it on the seventeenth-century antique vase in the front room – try an open drawer or a partially opened cupboard door and look for enough pressure to push it.

# Drop

*Time to train:* 3 weeks at 2 x sessions per day

*Type of trick:* Useful

*Application:* Asking your dog to drop things they shouldn't have will stop you from chasing them round the house like a crazed lunatic

*What you will need:* A lead and a selection of items that are unimportant to you but vary in value from your dog's point of view

This foundation trick comes in handy all the time, as will become apparent as you train your way through the book. It's also a really useful thing to teach your petulant pooch if they commonly take things that aren't theirs and then don't want to give them up!

1. There are lots of ways to teach this behaviour, and this way works for most dogs. Set yourself up with a small bowl of treats to one side. Pop your dog on the lead and give him a toy but only one he doesn't consider very valuable. The lead is there only to stop the dog from running off and burying it in the garden, not for anything else.

2. Once your dog has possession of the toy, say the word 'drop' and start dropping treats at your feet. If your dog immediately drops the toy and gobbles up the food let them keep the toy and ask them to get it again; have a little play and then repeat the whole process.

3. Some dogs won't want to leave it, so keep dropping treats away from their toy until they can't resist the draw of all the tasty morsels lying about on the floor. At this stage, do not attempt to pinch the toy before they can get it again, as that will make them suspicious of you and eventually ruin your cue.

4. What we are doing here is making it really attractive to spit out the object that's in the dog's mouth when they hear the word 'drop'. To do this we recommend doing lots and lots of repetitions of the above. At some point you'll notice that on the word 'drop' your dog simply lets go of the toy and waits for the food. Once you have noticed this change, move to the next step.

5. Say 'drop' and wait for your dog to spit the toy onto the floor. Mark this and give him lots and lots of treats. This time you are also going to get down to your dog's level and help him clear up all the treats by pointing them all out. This also gets the dog used to your hands coming near his stuff. Repeat this over a few sessions. For every five where you practise pointing out the treats, do one repetition where you actually pick the toy up while your dog finishes the treat. Once he has finished, have a little play with your dog before starting the process again.

6. Now move to harder items such as bones and chews and things he may have picked up in the park. Remember to keep practising with items that aren't valuable as well as things you genuinely want to take off your dog. Make

sure your dog has more experiences where he drops the item, gets the treats and then gets the item back than experiences where the item is taken off him.

7. Just keep in mind that the more you practise this in real life the better and more automatic the drop will be when you ask for it in training, or when it counts and your dog has taken something it would be dangerous for him to keep. This is one of those cues to add to your list of things to do every day with your dog.

# Hold

*Time to train:* 2 weeks at 2 x sessions per day

*Type of trick:* Useful

*Application:* This can be considered a skill that can form the basis of so many more tricks

*What you will need:* A selection of items that your dog can safely put in his mouth – paint rollers work exceptionally well for many dogs

When we are training tricks, the **drop** is only actually useful if they can hold first! We are now going to use a technique called **shaping**, and what you're looking for is five successful repetitions in a row before moving to the next step. When training your dog this is a useful rule you can stick to if in doubt. Sometimes we can over-egg the pudding, so to speak, and keep going and going on a step just because we aren't sure when or how to move the training closer to the goal. When this happens take a breather and, when you return, test to see that the dog gets it right five times in a row. If she does, then great! Now you just need to move that training on – so check back on your plan to see what the next step is.

1. Hold a soft toy out towards your dog – not in their face but close enough to ignite some interest. Whenever we train using props we need to make sure the dogs are comfortable with them. If I brought out a bone and stuck it in your face without letting you see and check it

first you would be none too happy! Make sure you offer your dog the same courtesy. As soon as they investigate the toy in any way, shape or form, click and treat.

2. This time mark when the dog actually makes contact with her nose on the toy. If she grabs it at this stage that's good news, so definitely jackpot her with lots of delicious treats. That said, when your dog does skip a step in training, don't assume they have mastered that step. Still mark and reward for any contact if they offer that on the next go. You can only skip a step if you are willing to bet us £50 that they will complete that step five times in a row – so, in this case, only move to the step where the

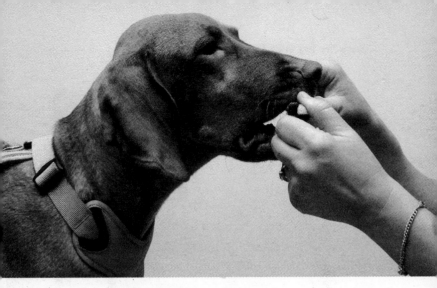

dog grabs it if they offer this five times in a row when you are just waiting for the contact.

3. Right, by now we can start clicking for the dog putting its mouth on the object. The toy will still be in our hands but, each time you re-present it, lower your hand towards the floor. Don't move to the next step until you can place the toy on the floor and the dog can grab it with their mouth. At this stage don't worry about whether they lift it or not – we are just coming to that!

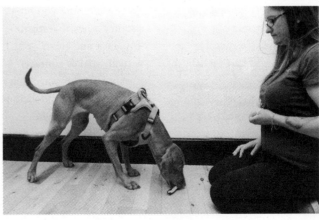

4.  Now you're looking for the toy to partially come off the ground. You can encourage the dog with lots of praise throughout this process but it's the marker that is the important part; if you mark too late you'll be teaching them to throw objects rather than hold them, so make sure that every click happens while the dog has the toy in her mouth. It's better to click early than late and it's better to not click at all than miss a click.

5.  This time we want at least five successful repetitions where the toy is lifted clean off the floor by the dog. Then mark while it's still in their mouth. Remember again about the timing of your marker. Can you now see why we insist on those games where you improve your timing by watching TV? So, if your dog runs in and picks up the toy but then drops it and you've

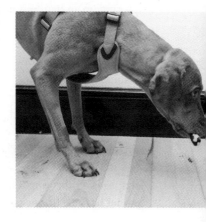

missed this epic pick-up, what do you do? Well, sadly, you don't mark. Because otherwise what happens is you end up confusing your dog because they won't know what got them the mark. If you feel like your timing is seriously off, spend the evening watching soaps and mark each time the camera angle changes – but make sure your dog is not in the room!

6. Step 6 is all about height – something we know very little about, being that we are both well below six feet. You want to gradually explain to your dog where you want the toy. So, you want the toy at the height where her head would usually be. Holding the toy but holding it down low isn't good enough. To break this down so our clever canine understands, the first five clicks will be for the toy coming off the ground for a minimum height of two inches. Then, after five successful repetitions, the following five holds need to be four inches off the floor to get a mark and a reward, then six inches, and so on until the dog picks up the toy and, if they were standing, it would be level with their spine.

7. Yay! We are at the point where your dog is coming in and picking up an item properly here. What awaits is a future of getting your dog to hold happy birthday messages for friends and bouquets of flowers at weddings. All that stands between you and this vision is a few steps of training, so hold tight.

First off, now that your dog clearly understands you want him to pick up and place an item in her mouth, you can bring in your cue word. We use 'hold' with our dogs but other common cues for this include 'take it' and 'get it'. With cue words, you want to choose something that rolls off the tongue so you don't forget it. Every dog owner has at least one cue that doesn't make sense to

the world around them. Jo uses 'this' as her heel cue and Nando uses 'pup-pup' as his recall cue. Don't worry if your cue ends up being something random – the words you use don't matter to the dog, so just use what comes out when you train.

So when you move to the next step, don't forget to cue your dog. The cue always comes first, as it tells the dog what's about to happen. So say 'hold' and then present the item to the dog.

8. This step is all about increasing the duration of the hold. What we mean by this is teaching your dog to actually hold it rather than run about with the toy or just pick it up and then drop it. From here on in you're going to get them to pick up the toy and, when they have it in their mouth level with their shoulders, count to two before clicking. Remember: if they drop it before you finish counting, don't click! Instead, pick up the toy and start over but maybe reduce the time that you're asking the dog to hold it for, so they are succeeding more than failing.

For the rest of this session you will increase the time they hold the object in increments of two seconds each go until they are holding the item on the cue hold for up to around ten seconds.

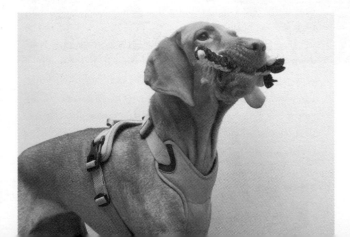

You can be as persistent as you like with this one. It is arguably one of the best foundations for cool tricks, so stick with it and make it slick and looking good before moving on to the next trick.

9. This is all about trying new objects with different textures, weights and smells to proof the behaviour, so that 'hold' doesn't only mean 'hold a soft toy' but you'll be able to point at nearly anything and ask your dog to hold it. Don't jump straight from a soft toy to a can or something really hard. A great tip is to play Kitchen Pickups, which is a game where you throw a bunch of friendly objects (recommendations include paint rollers, Sellotape roll, a bottle, a marker pen – things the dog can't swallow and won't chew. Now ask her to 'hold' each one as you go about your chores, cleaning up or cooking. Have a bowl of bacon bits and, for each item she holds for her time, mark and reward.

# Pull

*Time to train:* 5 days at 1 x session per day
*Type of trick:* Useful
*Application:* Another foundation skill that can be utilized in so many more advanced-level tricks
*What you will need:* Ribbon with knots tied in it

Getting your dog to pull with its mouth is a key skill used in many tricks. We've always found the most successful way of training this is to use ribbon as your initial teaching tool, although a fleece tug-toy can also work wonders for a more delicate mouth, or even a ball on a rope for dogs that struggle to put anything other than a ball in their mouth. You'll need to prepare your kit before you start. Take a length of ribbon approximately the length of your forearm and tie five knots equidistant from each other along its full length.

1. Start by making a concertina out of the knotted ribbon. Hold it in a fist with about two inches hanging out from between your forefinger and thumb and

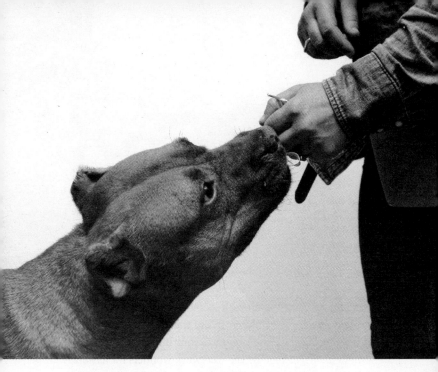

present this to the side of your dog's face. If you put it too close, the dog will lean away to avoid it, but get the distance right and they should lean in to investigate what it is you have in your hand. As soon as they show any interest, mark and reward.

2. Repeat Step 1 but this time around wait for the dog to actually make contact with the ribbon. To do this, ignore when the dog looks or investigates near the ribbon and wait for him to actually touch it. Repeat this until he has clearly demonstrated he knows that this game is all about the ribbon.

3. Now your dog should be showing keen interest in the ribbon and, with a little encouragement, they will want to nibble/grab/bite the ribbon. This is your new click point, which is just trainer code meaning this is what you are now pinpointing with your marker. You can encourage the dog by presenting it like a mouse in your

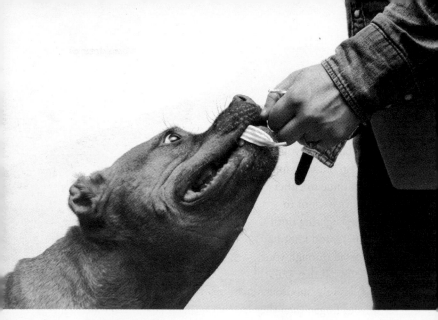

hand and making them a little excited by moving it through the air like it's trying to get away with its little tail trailing.

4. Repeat Step 3 but this time with a bit more enthusiasm. So this time, because we are after a fiercer grab, we need to make the thing they are chasing a bit fiercer too, so make the ribbon act as if it was a prey animal whipping its way across the floor to escape the big scary Pomeranian. At this point most dogs will leap into playing the big bad wolf and grab the ribbon. Don't click when they grab this time, though – hold off. Wait for them to enter a tug of war but you are only lightly gripping the ribbon by the knot closest to the dog. When the dog pulls the knot through your fingers, mark it and throw a sausage party!

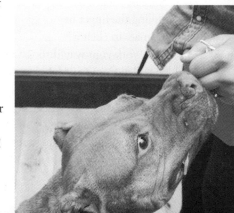

5. Repeat Step 4 but this time they not only have to pull one ribbon from your grasp but they must continue to either move back or to keep fighting until the second knot has passed through your hands. If they pull the  tail on the mouse hard enough to pull two knots through your finger, then they have won their mark and reward.

6. They should be starting to get the hang of it now, which means we should also be taking it easy on the dramatics element of prompting the dog to grab the ribbon. Make each game less and less exciting with less and less movement. Eventually this should look more like a suave gentleman gently undoing the lace corset of his lover and not a hooded teen pulling the finger of his mate to elicit a  fart. Work your way through until all five ribbons can be pulled from your hand with a minimal amount of exciting the dog.

7. You guessed it – time to bring in a cue. Ask your dog to 'pull' before presenting the ribbon to get all five knots pulled. Ta-da! Pull is on cue.

# A Trio of Tricks

*Time to train:* 3 weeks at 2 x sessions per day
*Type of trick:* Easy
*Application:* The warm-up!
*What you will need:* Nothing but patience and treats

The first trick we are going to start with is actually three separate tricks. Spin, twist and beg are three tricks used by many dog sports competitors as a way of warming up their dogs for more high-energy sports like agility, flyball and working trials. Not just that, but they are also fun ways to show off how smart your dog is down the dog park.

## Spin

The final goal of this trick is to have the dog turn a full 360-degree circle clockwise when you say the word 'spin'.

1.  We are going to use a technique known as **luring**. This is a hands-off method to manoeuvre a dog through or to a certain position. In this case we will take a treat and place it close to the nose of the dog. You'll know if you've got the right distance because the dog will follow the food. If your hand is too close the dog will snatch at the food; if your hand is too far away from the dog's nose then they will lose interest or

not move. Make sure you start with the dog in a standing position or they will end up in a heap on the floor.

Once we've ascertained the correct distance for the dog to follow the treat, slowly move your hand in a circular motion only a quarter of a circle. If the dog manages

to turn a quarter of the circle, then mark the behaviour with whatever marker you're using and follow by giving them the treat you have in your hand. We want to repeat this step five times with five correct responses before deciding to move up to the next level.

2. This step is going to be very similar except we are looking for half a circle from the dog. The size of your dog will dictate the style of your training. For a Chihuahua it will be effective to be on your knees with the dog in front of you; a Great Dane will need to be at your side while you're standing to allow you to move

your feet enough to make sure you can reach the full circumference of the circle. Again, five half-circles before you can lift your criteria.

3. Yep, that's it, you guessed it – three-quarters of a circle! This is the point where many dogs will start backing off. This is probably because you're leaning too far over the dog, which for some dogs can be quite intimidating or at best off-putting. Five in a row right and you're ready to make it a little harder.

4. You're now ready for the full circle! If you live with really big dogs, or you have arms that are comparable to Danny DeVito's, another technique is to train your dog to follow a target stick. This will give you a little extra length and make getting that full circle a bit easier.

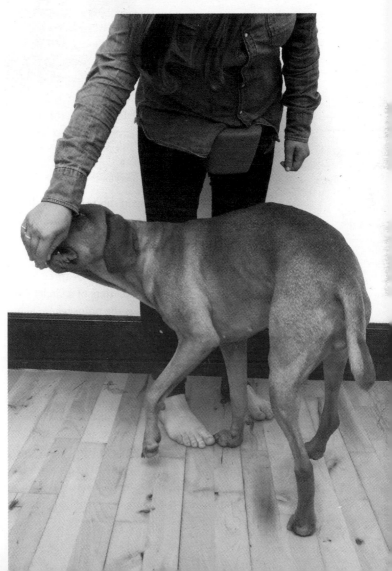

5. Fading the lure will be a common theme in this book. One of the most important things to remember when you're using a lure in dog training is that you need to fade it early. If you keep using it too long then the danger is it becomes part of what the dog expects in the trick, which makes it hard to train them to simply perform the trick when you ask. If that's the case, then you end up with a dog that needs to see the goods before they play any part in training with you. The simplest way to fade a lure is to have two treats – one in each hand. Lure the dog around full circle and mark the dog for reaching the right criteria but, this time, instead of feeding them the treat they were following, give them the treat from the other hand. Do this five times.

6. This time we're going back to having one treat, but this stays in the hand behind your back. Now you're going to attempt to lure the dog with an empty hand, but don't show them it's empty. Hold your hand exactly as you did

on the previous step and imagine you still have a treat in
your hand. If the dog successfully completes a full circle
after following your empty hand, mark it and reward
with food from behind your back. It also makes sense to
throw in a jackpot of three or four treats or an extra-long
game with their toy if they get it right, just to hammer
home the point that it still makes sense to listen to us
even if they can't see or smell food on us. This step is
vital for the dogs to realize that they don't have to see the
food for it to still be worth their while. As always, we're
aiming for a strong five reps before pushing our criteria.

7. Now we are going to add that all-important verbal cue –
a word you can use to explain to the dog what you want
them to do. By now you will have put a heavy history
of reinforcement behind the spin. That means the dog
has had a lot of experience of getting treats for spinning,
which makes it likely he will try it out again. We haven't
as yet muttered a word to tell the dog what to do, and
that's because we want the behaviour to be pretty close to
the finished product before giving it a word. The benefit

to this is that the mistakes we make in training won't be associated with the final word you use.

Here is the protocol for adding a word – what trainers call a cue – to any behaviour. First run through the behaviour to make sure the dog really knows what you're asking. Then stand still and say the cue word followed by whatever prompt or lure you're still using. From that moment on always say the word once, clearly, to ask the dog to perform.

So, in this case, after running the dog through the previous step, we will stand as still as possible, give the cue 'spin' and then lure the dog with an empty hand, as in Step 6, still paying with the reward from behind your back.

8.  Making the hand gesture smaller. We're really close to gold here but we want to make our big sweeping hand movement into more of a subtle hand signal. The way to achieve this is by slowly, with each passing repetition, making the hand signal a little smaller and smaller until you're happy with a gentle flick of the wrist and the word 'spin' to cue the dog to perform the final trick.

Teaching one trick at a time can become a little stale, so we prefer to spread our training across a few different sessions. Over the course of a week we may focus on teaching a couple of different tricks. Four or five sessions of 3–5 minutes will be spent teaching the dog how to spin. To make sure the dogs or ourselves don't get bored, we also spend the same amount of time teaching another trick. The second trick needs to be different enough as to not cause any confusion. It may not be sensible to teach a play dead and a roll over in the same week, as they are similar movements, but in this case a **spin** and a **beg** make for the perfect combination.

## Twist
The dog performs a full 360-degree circle in the opposing, anti-clockwise direction.

The twist is almost exactly the same as a spin apart from one obvious difference: the dog turns in the other direction. That means you can follow the same plan as above but just be aware that both you and the dog are going to find one direction easier than the other.

## Beg
The dog, from a sitting position, lifts its front paws up off the ground and keeps a steady position with the spine vertical to the floor on the cue of 'beg'.

This is one of those tricks that can be easy to train but it would be wise spending weeks teaching it to help your dog develop the core muscles required to hold its body in an upright position. This is really only suitable for your dog if they have stopped physically growing, so give this one a miss if you have a puppy or adolescent dog.

55

1. Make sure your dog starts this trick from the sitting position. So, ask for the sit and, if your dog breaks the position whilst you are luring, remove the lure and ask for the sit again. Your dog will soon realize that they need to stay in a sit for the fun training games to continue.

   Take a treat between your forefinger and thumb and place it close to your dog's nose. Imagine there is an invisible piece of thread running from your dog's nose to your treat and use this to slowly lift their head up like a puppet. As soon as the dog lifts their head, mark it with your clicker or your marker word and then give them the treat. Try to get at least three successful repetitions in a row and then push to the next step. If you only get one or two correct responses in a row, start counting your three reps again.

2. Repeat as before, but this time just a head going up isn't close enough to our final goal. This time we are going to look for one of the pup's paws to leave the floor. Mark as soon as any paw lifts off the floor to get to that treat. Then feed – ideally when the paw is still off the floor.

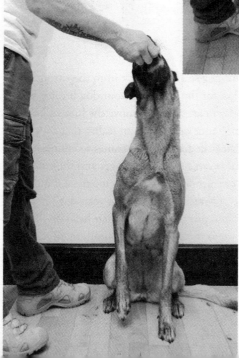

3. Once your dog is nailing one paw off each time, you can begin to expect both front paws to leave the floor. Mark the exact moment both are in the air, even if it's only for a fraction of a second, and even if it's only a tiny bit off the surface of the floor.

4. We're going to expect a little more from the dogs each time we go up a step, so this time we will expect both front paws to have left the floor for a count of two seconds before we click and treat. Remember to get your three-in-a-row right because if you jump a step it's likely you'll get unstuck towards the end of the trick. Even if your dog does better than you expect and jumps a few steps without you trying, mark it, reward it heavily but don't expect it on the next go.

5. At this point we want to start adding distractions to our training. The temptation for most would be to keep building the time that the dog can stay in position, but this doesn't allow for much conditioning of the core muscles. Remember the golden rule: happy and healthy! The best way to make sure we stick to that rule is to add at least four new steps with different distractions. This time around you're going to get your dog's front feet off the floor but, during the count to two seconds, try to sidestep your left leg out to the side and bring it back

in. If your dog is still in the position when you've finished your surprise dance move, then mark and reward and don't forget to praise them too.

6. Same as before but without the leg kick, this time you're going to lift one of your arms above your head and then drop it back to your side all within the two count. We're not looking to extend the time just yet, although the arm up might take a little longer than the leg lift.

7. This time we are going to up the ante a little. While your dog is in the beg position, you're going to turn a 360-degree circle in front of them. This can be quite a challenge, as dogs have the tendency to seek out your face, so do it too slow and your dog is likely to break the position. Remember to get your three-in-a-row right before you go up a step. How you choose

to style the spin is up to you. Jo tends to opt for the ballerina-type pirouette, whereas Nando usually pulls off a slick Michael Jackson impression.

8. Keeping in line with our spins, your goal for this step is going to be a tough one. We want you to try walking a full circle around your dog. Many dogs will struggle with this step, so be patient and, if you fail too often, try feeding the dog in position as you pass behind them. You can do this by feeding as soon as  he is in position then taking a few steps and feed. And another few steps and reward. Then each time you take the circle, cut down how many treats you feed him until you can walk around the whole dog in the beg without feeding a treat until the end.

9. Start building up the duration for the amount of time the dog can hold the position. Slowly increase the time and, if you're brave enough, once you get to eight seconds throw in some new distractions of your choosing.

# Roll Over

**The dog will drop into a down then roll over a full circle on its back**

*Time to train:* 3 weeks at 1 x session every 2 days
*Type of trick:* Confidence builder
*Application:* Vet visit
*What you will need:* Lots of small tasty treats

If the vet ever needs to inspect the belly of your dog, then getting them to roll over is one way to get there without having the stress of pinning them down. You'll only need a little more training to keep them on their back exposing their belly. Plus it makes for a cool party trick!

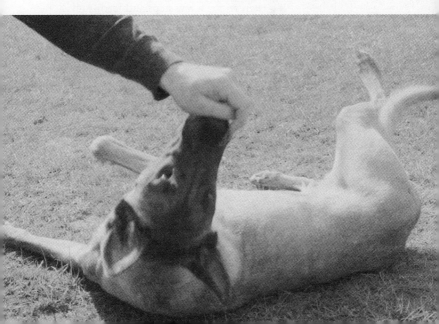

You'll need somewhere suitable to practise this trick – a carpeted floor or a yoga mat makes for comfortable practice, but a sofa can actually hinder your progress because it's too soft. Concrete or tiled flooring won't work because it will be cold and likely uncomfortable for your beloved dog.

1. From a down position, where your dog is lying like a Sphinx, take a treat out and lure their head around to one side. Move the food slowly to keep them focused on the reward and try to keep it at nose level, running horizontally with the floor. This should cause them to flop onto one hip. Always go in the direction they have decided to rest upon – it will be much easier for both of you. Once they drop on the hip, click and treat.

2. From the flop, try moving the lure over the back of the
   dog in a half-crescent shape. For them to reach this
   they have to perform some funky moves and, if you're
   moving your hand slowly enough, they will eventually
   expose their belly. This is the point to reward with
   lashings of treats!

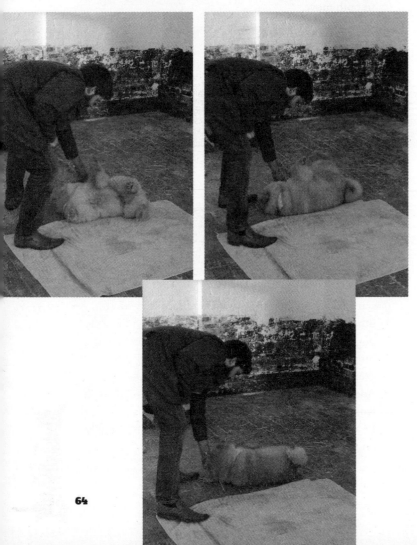

3.  Once you've got the dog to the point where they will happily roll over and expose their stomach, you'll want to follow the half-moon all the way to the floor and then draw it out towards you. This should cause the dog to flip all the way over and back into the down position. Practise this until they can do the full roll over in one smooth move.

4.  Now it's time to remove that pesky lure. We will use the same trick as before: a treat in each hand. And, just like before, lure your dog over with one hand but pay with the other. Just like we've used on previous tricks, we can start having no lure in one hand and feeding with the other, then work up to no lures at all and just luring the dog with the point. Once the dog is consistently being lured to roll over, you can bring in a cue word then eventually lose the lure.

5.  Add your cue, 'Roll over', and remember to try to say the word first before you lure the dog. Over time you should be able to reduce the lure until your dog will roll simply on the verbal cue word.

# Tricks That Are Simpler Than They Seem

# Ring a Bell

**Dog rings a dinner bell when asked**

*Time to train:* 1 week at 1 x session per day
*Type of trick:* Easy
*Application:* Ring a bell can be a cute trick or can be used to
let your dog communicate he needs the toilet
*What you will need:* A push-button bell

This trick, although funny to watch, can actually have very
useful applications. Some people have been known to train
their dogs to ring a bell when they need the toilet, so they
can let them out into the garden. It even works for little
puppies, avoiding many toilet-training mistakes when the
pups need to go, know where to go, but don't know how to
communicate that need to their human.

1.  Take your dog's
    favourite food,
    show them a
    piece and place it
    underneath the
    bell. Make sure it's
    small enough so the
    dog can't get to it
    straight away and it
    doesn't prevent the
    bell from ringing.

Keep your hand on the edge of the bell if you have a big oaf of a dog – this should stop them kicking it across the room – but if your pooch is more of a light-footed princess then it's OK to just let the dog explore the bell with their keen sense of smell. It's likely they will try out a few different tactics to get to the food – these might include scratching the floor next to the bell, pushing it with their nose and maybe even barking at it. It's your job to ignore all of the above and wait till the dog makes any contact with their paw to the bell. Capture the moment this happens with your clicker and lift the bell

so the dog can access the food hidden underneath. Aim for ten strong correct repetitions in a row before moving to the next step.

2. Because we're using a lure for this trick, we need to remember to fade that out of the context as quickly as possible. This time pretend to hold a treat in your hand and place the imaginary treat under the bell – because the dog has just practised ten reps in a row, he is likely to do the same behaviour that worked for him previously. As soon as the paw touches the bell, mark and treat.

3. We're now going to be a little pickier with how the dog hits the bell, rather than accepting any old contact.
   The easiest way to make sure we are accepting the same standard each time is to wait for the bell to ring. If it rings, pup gets a biscuit. But no sound, no food.
4. Add the cue for the bell by having it out of reach in your hands, saying, 'Ring it' and then placing it down.

Top tip: between training sessions make sure the bell is packed away out of reach. The last thing you want the dog to do is continually activate the bell and not get rewarded. This could have the same effect as you putting money into a broken vending machine; after a couple of attempts you're likely to stop feeding money into a machine that doesn't work. If the dog believes the bell doesn't work because he has attempted it one too many times while you're out of earshot, he too will stop ringing it altogether!

# Turn on the Light

**Dog switches light on or off when asked**

*Time to train:* 2 weeks at 1 x session per day
*Type of trick:* Household help
*Application:* Trained dogs are waiting to help us, so give
     them a job!
*What you will need:* Lamp with a floor switch

Imagine getting home after a long walk with the dog and
falling down on the sofa to pick up this book but alas there is
a problem! It's too dark to read it and you're too tired to get
up and switch on the reading lamp. Fear not, because your
clever little pooch can come running over and hit the floor
switch. You get to read the best book you've ever bought and
they get to cuddle up on the sofa with you while you do it.

    This trick is surprisingly similar to the 'ring a bell' trick
and, if you teach it soon after, your dog will find it a breeze.
Because the tricks are so similar we will write a summary
below but, if you get stuck, don't be afraid to check out the
'ring a bell' steps to help you troubleshoot.

1. Put a treat under the floor switch and hold it down.
   Allow the dog to investigate and make attempts to
   get the food – now mark and reward any contact with
   the paw on the light switch. Repeat this until you are
   confident the dog understands that paw on the switch is
   what is driving the behaviour.

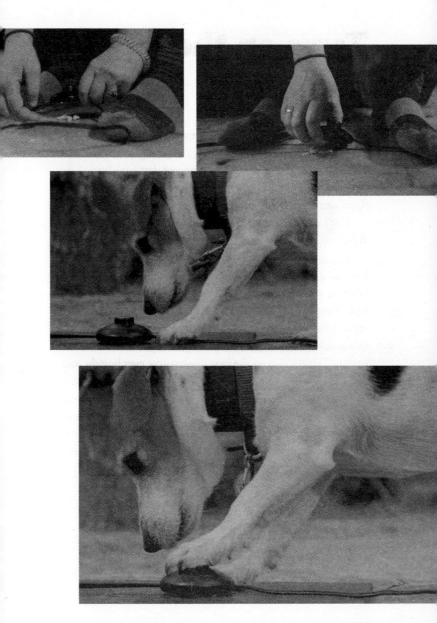

2. This time you're going to pretend to put a treat under the switch. Let the dog have a look and see if they can guess they still need to scratch to get their click and treat. Remember you are still marking for the paw hitting the switch.
3. Now start rewarding only the paw touches that have enough pressure to actually turn the lights on or off. So that mark will happen when the light changes status. Remember if that doesn't happen, you don't click and treat, but if the dog tries five times in a row and fails all five times, stop and check that the switch isn't too hard for him.
4. When you have got to the stage where your dog knows to press the switch until the light changes each time, you can now add your cue. 'Switch' is what we use.
5. Step 5 can work for any of the tricks, but it is particularly important with this one, otherwise you end up with a dog who spends all day switching the lights on and off in a relentless bid for food! So play a game where you reward the dog a couple of times when you guys walk around close by the lamp but don't switch it. Then reward the dog again and cue it.

# Wipe Your Feet

**The end goal is to be able to ask our dogs to wipe their own feet when they come in from a muddy walk in the woods**

*Time to train:* 3 weeks at 1 x session per day
*Type of trick:* Household help
*Application:* No more dirty paw prints
*What you will need:* Tough floor mat

The benefits are obvious! No more grief from the other half about 'them bloomin' dogs'! The training plan is very similar to the 'ring a bell' trick, so we will keep this one brief.

1. Show the dog a reward they love and then place it under the mat. Stand on the mat with your feet at the edges to keep it in place. Allow the dog to do its thing, but this time you're looking for any scratching/digging behaviour on the mat. Once you spot it, mark and reward.

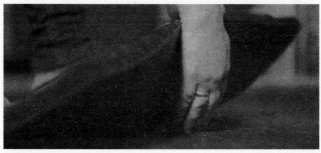

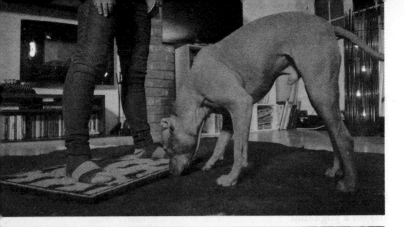

2.  Now just pretend to put the goods under the mat, wait for the scratch, click, treat and repeat.

3.  When you're willing to bet us £20 that as soon as you put the mat down the dog will go over and dig at it, then you're ready to add a cue. Remember the cue comes before anything else on every repetition. So ask for 'wipe your feet' and then mark and reinforce the dog each time for performing the foot scratching.

# Dog Yoga

**Dog goes into a bow position (elbows on floor, bum in air) on a yoga mat**

*Time to train:* 2 weeks at 1 x session per day
*Type of trick:* Party piece
*Application:* A great way to impress your guests at the end of a dinner party
*What you will need:* Nothing but treats

This isn't the daft yoga with dogs that you may have seen where people lift their dogs into all kinds of crazy positions; this is about teaching postures that are beneficial for the wellbeing of your dog. The bow, in many cases, is associated with play. Remember when I said the dog shouldn't be able to tell the difference between play and training?

1. Take a treat, place it in the palm of your hand and cover it with your thumb. Starting with your dog in a standing position, place your thumb with the treat underneath their nose and point your fingers at their back paws. Imagine there is a rail running from their nose to the paws – you're going to move the treat along that rail.

   The dog will likely lean back without moving their front paws – click, this is exactly what we are looking for. On each rep you're looking for the elbows to bend and the chest to lower to the floor but the bum should be up in the air, tail wagging!

2. We're going to go back to using two treats to help us fade the lure, so don't forget to feed with the treat from behind your back. Hold one treat to lure, then mark when the dog has pulled down. Now allow the dog to collect his prize from the other hand.

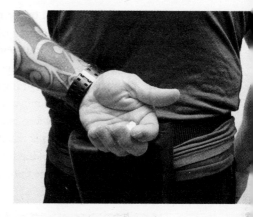

3. Once Fido has managed to accomplish a few bows with the treat coming from your other hand, let's try with no treat in your hand at all. Make sure he gets lashings of praise followed by some delicious goodies if he is still able to pull down into the bow.

4. Introduce your cue. I use the words 'Ta da' and bow myself, but you get to pick whatever you desire! Pick the cue – ask your dog, 'Bow?' and now lure using the empty food hand to pull your pooch into position. Over the next ten repetitions of this, slowly reduce how much you are using your arm until your dog needs no prompting or signalling and can drop straight into posture on a verbal cue word!

Now, after all that work you really should take a bow.

# Medium-
level Tricks

# Medium-level Tricks

# Hoop Jump

*Time to train:* 6 weeks at 1 x session per day
*Type of trick:* Fun
*Application:* Getting your dog fit through tricks
*What you will need:* Hula hoop

This trick calls for your dog to be healthy, a good weight and with good joints. If you're not sure about this or if you have any concerns, go and speak to your vet. You're going to need a hula hoop and somewhere soft for the dog to land, so the garden is a good place to start.

1. Hold the hula hoop vertically with the bottom part of the hoop resting on the floor. Have your dog sitting on one side and then take out a treat and reach through from the other. As your dog follows the food through, wait for their whole body to pass through and then toss the treat in the direction they are moving. Practise this a few times in both directions.

2. Lift the hoop a couple of inches off the floor and try again. This time your dog will have to hop a little to get through without tripping over; as soon as they hop mark it yes and toss

**83**

the food. If your dog is on the larger side they probably haven't even noticed, so you're going to lift the hoop after every rep by an inch or two until they do hop!

While you're practising this, you're also going to try less luring and more pointing through the hoop. For each repetition try to ensure the hoop increases in height – just a tiny bit – and the hand lure reduces just a tiny bit also. As long as you mark the dog in the air and reward on the other side in the direction of travel, you should end up fading the lure without much of a problem.

3. Jumping can be quite energy consuming for some dogs, so make sure you don't overdo it when it comes to your training sessions, especially as you are getting higher and

higher jumps. The higher the jump, the higher the value of the reward you'll need to deliver!

How much you increase the height of your jump depends a lot on the size of your dog. Small dogs can cope easily with an inch at a time and larger dogs should be capped at around 1ft per jump. Slowly build up the height over sessions.

4. If you want to be really flash you can get rid of the hoop
   and teach your dog to dive head first through a hoop made
   by your arms. Now this one *will* impress your friends!

   Start by holding the hoop in two hands rather than
   one and, with each jump, slowly move your hands
   towards each other around the hoop. Unless you have
   the arms of an ape, there will likely come a point where
   you can't reach any further around the hoop, and at this
   point discard the hoop but pretend as if you're holding it.
   Encourage your dog through, but make sure you make a
   big deal of it if they get it right!

5. For smaller dogs you can slowly make your arms
   into a full hoop for them to jump, but try this with a
   Doberman and, at the very best, you'll end up in a heap
   on the floor, laughing at yourself. Don't forget to add the
   cue word. We say 'hoopla' as our word to tell our dogs
   what to do.

# Open the Door

*Time to train:* 6 weeks at 1 x session per day

*Type of trick:* Household help

*Application:* Get the dog to open the door when your hands are full of shopping

*What you will need:* Grab a tug-toy, some ribbon and plenty of treats

Opening the door on cue can be useful. You can use it to ask your dog to open not just doors, but also drawers, washing machines and fridges. In the summer it can be especially useful when 'open the fridge' is joined to another behaviour such as 'fetch the gin, the tonic and a lime'!

For your dog to be able to open a door, they'll first need to know how to pull a length of ribbon – but your dog already knows this, right? You didn't jump to this trick without teaching the basics first, did you?

1. Attach the ribbon to a door handle. We will be describing the trick as if we were using it on the type of door handle common on many interior doors in homes, with a handle that sits horizontal, which you grasp and turn vertically to open the door.

Once the ribbon is attached, call your dog over while you hold onto the ribbon and verbally encourage your dog to pull on the ribbon. Accept any attempt to pull for the first few times; we do this because changing the context of the situation could cause all kinds of confusion depending on how sensitive they are.

2. This time expect your dog to pull the ribbon without you holding on to it. Over the course of the next ten repetitions, see if you can move your hand further and further away, still giving encouragement and pointing at the ribbon to prompt him.

3. Once Step 2 is complete, start marking and rewarding only those attempts that actually pull on the handle strongly enough for it to move the handle down. To do this you will need to slowly up the ante – first marking any movement, then any

movement a quarter down, then half, then three-quarters, until you are only marking on a full pull down.

4. From now on we will only reward the dog if his strength is good enough to actually open the door.

Caution: remember to remove your ribbon between training sessions so your dog doesn't just let themselves in or out whenever they like!

5. If you want to make this trick something really exceptional then you can add the cue of a ringing doorbell. The way to do this is to get the help of a friend to press the bell – or some more modern bells can be rung from a remote.

Set up your session the same as you did in all the other steps but this time you have the remote handy. Start close to the door and only move further away when your dog is confidently getting it right. Press the bell and then encourage your dog to open the door by pointing. After several reps the dog will make the association between the sound of the bell and the behaviour that gets rewarded, but here's the important part. To really hammer home the idea that Fido should open the door only when the doorbell goes off, you need to set the dog up without pressing the bell, and if he opens it nothing bad happens but nothing good happens either. In the end the dog will realize that opening the door when the bell goes off will earn him a reward but doing it without the sound of the bell will not earn him anything.

# Close the Cupboard

*Time to train:* 3 weeks at 1 x session per day
*Type of trick:* Household help
*Application:* Getting help around the house is one job our dogs will be happy to help with, and all for some treats!
*What you will need:* Post-it notes

Once you've trained this trick you'll be able to send in your faithful canine companion to tidy up after your non-compliant teenager. And since we have already taught our pooch to open a door it would be bad manners if he didn't know how to shut it on his way out.

1. Your dog has already learnt how to target a Post-it note and that will come in handy! To start this trick, do a few reps with the Post-it. Practise and make sure your dog is really giving it a good nudge before moving on to Step 2.
2. Stick the note to the door. This set of ten is all about slowly moving your hand away and building in a pointing gesture. The way to do this is to have your hand next to the note and encourage your dog to touch it. If they touch your hand then nothing happens, but if they touch the note then good stuff happens! Over the course of the session slowly move your hand further and further away from the note.

3. Have the cupboard door slightly ajar and accept any push that actually moves the door, even if it's only a fraction and it doesn't shut to start with.

4. From now on we want the door to shut completely. So the next few stages will only be marked if the door shuts.
   - Five reps with the door open three inches.
   - Five reps with the door open six inches.
   - Five reps with the door halfway open.
   - Five reps with the door three-quarters open.
   - Five reps fully open.

5. Now add your cue. We use 'close it' because 'shut it!' is a bit too *EastEnders*! Say 'close it' before pointing to the cupboard. Now that your dog is closing the door on cue, it's time to get rid of those ugly Post-it prompts. To do this, have a practice session getting your dog to close the door on cue but rip the Post-it in half and practise five repetitions.

   Now rip the Post-it in half again and practise another five reps. And again and again until there is no Post-it on the door whatsoever.

If you're feeling brave, start attempting multiple doors on one cue. Simply open a few doors and start by saying 'close it'. Once your dog has finished, merely point at the next door before clicking and treating.

# Retrieve Your Lead

*Time to train:* 3 weeks at 1 x session per day
*Type of trick:* Calming
*Application:* Calm dog can equal a calm walk
*What you will need:* Your hand and some tasty treats!

When dogs leave the house in a state of excitement for their walk it can cause a whole list of problems, from pulling on the lead to lunging and barking at other dogs. We recommend that people increase mental stimulation for their dogs and, if it's a trick that can also be helpful, well, that's good news for everyone. This trick can also build a routine that will reduce excitement around the walks by keeping that mutt's mind busy! This involves your dog running away from you to fetch their lead and bringing it back to you so you can take them out for a walk.

1.  Set yourself up with a pile of tasty treats, your dog's lead, a clicker and somewhere comfortable to sit. Once you're ready then present the lead out in front of your dog. If they investigate it at all, click and treat. If they don't, try rubbing a little bit of the food on the lead so they are more likely to give it a sniff next time. Mark each investigation. Five successful reps of this is enough to get to the next step.

2.  Hold the lead out again but, this time, for the dog to earn a click, the lead must touch their lips – even if it's by accident you still mark and reward. That doesn't mean that you move the lead and touch it on the dog's lips, though. It's really important that you wait it out until the dog comes and gives the lead a little kiss themselves.

3.  You're going to need to be patient here, but stop clicking the dog for touching the lead with their lips and wait them out to get their teeth on it. Holding the lead out tightly for the dog can help prompt this. As soon as those teeth touch the lead you're going to pay your dog in treats.

4.  Repeat Step 3 but without holding the lead. Put it on the floor instead or, if your dog finds it easier, put it on a chair. Remember: any tooth contact with the lead gets a reward. Ideally the dog will approach the lead and mouth it, then return to you for a treat.

5.  Now the dog is happily biting at the lead we are going to expect some of the lead to come off the floor. The best way to do this is to tie it into a bundle, just like they do with mountain-climbing ropes. This will make it slightly easier for the dog to pick up without tripping over it.

6.  Once your dog is comfortably lifting the lead each and every time, we are going to try to time the click for when the lead actually completely leaves the ground. If

the dog can pick up the entire lead and you can see any daylight between the lead and the floor, then mark and reward.

7. Step 6 will need to be repeated a dozen or so times, so it's really slick and your canine companion knows exactly what to do. With the dog happily putting the lead in their mouth, we need to teach them to give it to us. As we've already taught the hand target at the start, when we learnt the foundations, this should be easy. The moment they have the lead in their mouth, cue them to 'touch' your hand and, hopefully, you'll be well on your way to the end goal. When you start this part, make sure you are right next to your dog but, as time goes on and he becomes more and more confident, start moving further and further away.

8. Now you're going to start practising in the location where the lead is normally kept and, if your dog gets it right, you're going to use the functional reward of taking them out for a walk as well as treating them.

So, simply point towards the lead and start adding your cue. Say, 'Fetch the lead' and wait for your perfect pooch to go and retrieve his lead. Because you've changed the association with the lead from crazy outside madness to a more calm and thoughtful association, you should find your walk just a little more manageable from the get-go too. As soon as your dog retrieves his lead on cue, clip him on, give him a treat and go on a little trek.

# Leg Weave

We worked with the talented tricksters and winners of
*Britain's Got Talent*, Ashley and Pudsey, and they showed us
at Pet School that the leg weave is a very cool-looking trick
and your dog is totally capable of being just as cool! The dog
will weave in and out of your legs in a figure of eight while
you stand still. If you've got little legs and a big dog, make
sure you film the process and post it to social media with the
hashtag #teachmypet! We always welcome a giggle.

1. Start with your dog in a sitting position in front of you. Now, with a treat in your hand, reach around behind you and then between your legs and lure your dog through your legs. As they come out of the other side, mark the behaviour and reward the dog.

2. Now they're happy with walking through your legs, it's time to start moulding them into the famous YouTube star they can be. Start as above but, once they start walking through your legs, keep the treat moving but bend it, keeping it tight to your right leg until it's on your kneecap, then mark and reward.

3. This time around you'll need two treats, one in each hand. The first one is given at the knee and the second is gently rolled between your legs so it bounces off behind you, hopefully with Fido in hot pursuit.

4. Still two treats, first one at the knee and then, as they move to get what they think will be a rolling treat, you will lure them around your left leg and feed them on your left kneecap. To do this you will have to master the skill of feeding your first treat while reaching behind you with your left hand to be ready to lure them through again.

5. Repeat Step 4 but pretend to have a treat in your right hand. Make sure you still pay them when they reach your left knee, though!

6. No treats in your hands, get the full figure of eight and then jackpot them with a special treat if they make it all the way round.

7. As always, we don't label it until we love it! Add your
   cue; it can be whatever you fancy. Remember: dogs don't
   speak English, so we can use something that's easy to
   recall, like 'weave', or we can be a little more obscure and
   use 'banana' as our cue – it really doesn't matter as long
   as we are consistent. Oh, but don't get cross if you offer
   someone a banana and your dog trips you up!

**Hard
Tricks**

# Hard
# Tricks

# Fetch a Beer From the Fridge

*Time to train:* 8 weeks at 1 x session per day
*Type of trick:* Chain of previously trained behaviours
*Application:* Impressive
*What you will need:* Fridge, beer and ribbon

If you've spent your time working through the tricks in
this book, you're going to find it starts to really pay off
because many of the more advanced tricks will utilize
movements and techniques that your dog will have
already practised.

The 'fetch a beer from the fridge' trick is broken down
into several different behaviours. The dog will have to go to
the fridge, pull open the door, hold a beer can, target your

hand, drop the beer and then return to the fridge to close the door. Teaching these individual elements isn't the hard part, although it is time-consuming chaining the behaviours together so they are all carried out on one cue – that's where the real challenge lies.

So let's break all those behaviours down.

### Open the Door

You've taught this as a trick in its own right, so I'll give you a summary to follow:

1. Teach the dog to pull a ribbon through your hand (check back to the 'pull' trick).
2. Tie the ribbon to the fridge and reward the dog for pulling the ribbon on cue.

### Hold

Teaching your dog to hold a beer can will depend a lot on the size of your dog. If you own a small dog like a Chihuahua, then you're going to need to adapt the trick and the can to suit your dog. We will be describing the trick for a

medium-sized dog but tying something to the ring-pull can work for some small dogs, and using a mini-fridge on the floor – so they aren't trying to move mountains just to open the door – can also help.

Take a beer can and wrap it in gaffa tape; you want there to be about five layers of thickness on the can. This is going to help the dog get some purchase, and will also make it easier for more sensitive dogs that don't like the feeling of metal in their mouth.

Play with the can as if it were a toy, hiding it from the dog and whipping it away until the dog has some serious interest in it, then roll it along the floor. If your dog runs over and pounces on it, mark it and reward it. Many dogs will pick the can up straight away, so swap the can for their favourite thing, be it toys or food.

Keep playing with the can and, each session, take off another layer of gaffa tape. This needs to be built up to the point where you can wind your dog up while holding his harness after having already placed the can on the seat of a chair. Cue them to 'get it' and release the harness. If they run out and grab it, then you'll be more likely to succeed when it comes to chaining the behaviours together.

## Target Your Hand

This is another trick that we've already taught during the 'close the cupboard' exercise, so I'll write a brief summary.

1. Post-it note on the hand presented to the side of the face. Reward any investigation.
2. Start rewarding any nose-to-note contact.
3. Fade the target by tearing the Post-it note in half and then making it progressively smaller until the dog is happily pushing his nose into your hand.

## Close the Fridge

Again, the dog should have the idea of this if you practise some of the steps of 'close the cupboard' but with the Post-it note stuck to the fridge door.

1. Click and treat for nose to Post-it note.
2. Transfer Post-it to the fridge door.
3. Incrementally open the door further until it is fully open, remembering to only reward the dog for fully closing the fridge door.

There you have all the elements to a rather complicated trick, but now we will teach the dog to link all of those behaviours together with a process called **chaining**.

The first step is to pair up the behaviours.

## Pull Open + Hold

Start next to the fridge and ask the dog to tug the ribbon. As soon as they have the door open, point at the beer, which you've placed in a drawer in the door low enough for the dog to reach without any major complications. If you really want to set the dog up for success, make sure there is no chicken, cake, sausage or anything else in the fridge that your dog would really like to get stuck into – or, at the very least, make sure it's not at nose level. If they do scoff something, you can't blame them; you were warned!

If your dog picks out the beer can, make a big deal out of it and give them tons of praise and a good selection of treats.

## Hold + Touch

This time we are going to ask the dog to hold the beer can while it's in front of you. When they pick it up, present the flat of your palm out to the side and then ask

them to touch. And bam! You just cheated your way to a beer-can retrieve!

## Touch + Push Closed

On this session we're going to ask your dog to do a hand touch followed by closing the fridge door. Make sure you start close to the fridge but still being fussy enough about the door closing. If the dog makes too many mistakes, look at having the door on the fridge nearly closed to get a few good reps in.

Now we have them all covered you're going to work your way through them all but backwards.

1. Push Closed
2. Touch + Push Closed
3. Hold + Touch + Push Closed
4. Open + Hold + Touch + Push Closed

Over the course of a few sessions, build up the distance till you can do it from the sofa and drop out the occasional cue, only adding the prompts for the next part of the sequence if your dog needs help.

Once it's becoming more and more reliable, add your cue! And voila, you have the coolest dog on the block.

# Tidy Up Your Toys

*Time to train:* 8 weeks at 1 x session per day

*Type of trick:* Useful

*Application:* You feed, love and walk them, so the least our dogs can do is tidy up after themselves!

*What you will need:* Selection of toys and a box for them to go in

This is one of the best tricks to teach your dog if you're houseproud. On the cue of 'tidy up', your dog will run out and find all his toys and drop them back into his toy box. Obviously your dog is going to need his or her very own toy box.

Once again, the skills your dog has learnt over the course of the book are going to come in handy here, too. We're going to chain together many previously taught behaviours to make one very impressive trick.

## The Breakdown

- Pick up the toy – hold
- Orientate to the box – target
- Drop

1. Let's start with picking up the toy. If your dog has been through the 'fetch a beer' trick, then picking up one of their own toys will be a simple task in comparison. Wave the toy around, get your dog excited and then slide it around on the floor, allowing your dog to chase it. Just

before you roll it out in front of you, use the words 'get it' and either play with your dog when they pounce on the toy or drop them a selection of five treats (whichever they prefer).

2. Once the dog is happily grabbing his toy, try dropping it near the box and, the moment they pick it up, cue the target and point at the Post-it note you have stuck on the inside of the toy box. If they touch the Post-it note with their nose while holding the toy, mark it and drop some treats in the box. This will encourage your dog to keep heading in the right direction and, as a by-product, they will have to drop the toy.

3. Now we have them happily picking up a toy, it's time to add two toys and, with each successful session, add another until they can tidy up four or five in a row. The next step is to start to engage their superpower: their sense of smell. We are going back to using only two toys for this part of the training. One will be out in the middle of the floor and the other will be out of sight

but easy to reach and nearby, maybe tucked around the side of the sofa. Prompt the dog to 'get it' and reward them for bringing back the first toy as per usual but, once they have eaten their spoils, immediately ask them to get it again and point in the general direction of the toy. They will look and then start to sniff out the toy; once they drop it in the box, reward them. It will seem extraordinary to us but, as far as your dog is concerned, this is the most natural thing in the world. However, getting them to find their toys uses a lot of mental energy, so expect them to be worn out. Bonus!

Remember that as you practise you can start moving further away from the box until your dog will run off to get the toys and pop them in the box while you can sit with your coffee on the sofa!

4. As time goes on you can increase the amount of toys your dog has to pick up and bring to the box in order to earn his treats. Ask your dog to 'get it', then, once he's put it in the box, ask him to get it again. Mark and reward once the dog has got both toys in the box. You can slowly start to increase this so your dog is tidying all of his toys on one cue!

# Hop On – Walking on Your Feet

*Time to train:* 8 weeks at 1 x session per day
*Type of trick:* Party piece
*Application:* There is literally nothing useful about this trick; it just looks cool
*What you will need:* No specialist equipment needed apart from maybe longer legs

Getting your dog to walk between your legs like you're a commando is a trick all unto itself. We call it the peek-a-boo position, but we're going to take it one step further than that and get them to walk on your toes, so you're actually getting two tricks for the price of one here!

1. Lure your dog between your legs so that you're facing the same direction. This is harder than it sounds, so you'll be happy you spent that extra time at the beginning teaching them to follow the food lure. Once they're in place you can keep feeding them as long as they stay there.

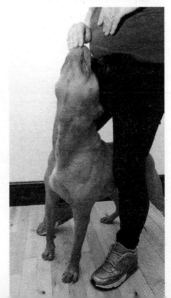

2. This time, once you get them in position, feed them a treat. Feed the treat from above so that it comes from the upside-down V of your legs and then take a half-step forward; they will likely rejoin you, and you repeat, taking small steps forward after every treat.

3. Now they're happy with moving, we're going to make it easier by standing still again – but you're going to take off your shoes. That's right, you heard us – take off your shoes, stand with your feet just over shoulder-width apart, or as far as your dog needs, depending on how big they are. Place your shoes or grab some old trainers (probably best to steer clear of expensive high-heels) in between your feet, facing in the same direction  as you with the tips of the shoes touching and the heels pointing away from each other. Once you're there, lure the dog back into the peek-a-boo position and try to manoeuvre the treat so you make the dog shift his weight onto one leg. Now watch the other leg and click for any contact with that paw and the shoe on the same side. If the paw makes contact, they get a treat; if the dog stands

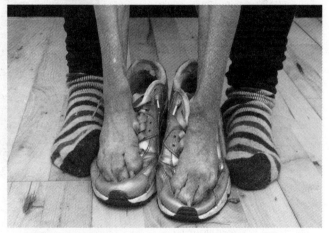

on the shoe then it keeps getting paid while it keeps its foot there.

4. You have one foot comfortably standing on a shoe. Your task this time is to put the dog's body weight on the shoe it's standing on, so you can move the other foot onto the other shoe. This takes some serious luring skills, so be patient and, if you get frustrated, just take a break. Two paws on shoes = sausages.

5.  Repeat the entire process above again, but this time you're going to gradually move the shoes apart until they are where your feet started. Once they are, slip your feet into the shoes.

6. This is all about getting your dog used to movement while standing on your feet, so start by wiggling your toes, then lift one foot a tiny bit, then take a step forward and continue this until you can walk – although it's unlikely to be very gracious. If your dog stays put, feed them a treat with every movement.

Well done! You now have an awesome little menu of tricks your dog can demo for your friends and family, which also help him keep mentally stimulated. If you've worked your way through all of these tricks then you are no longer a rookie in the trick-training world; you could almost be considered a trick-dog ninja! You will also have noticed the endless benefits to training your dog, such as deeper communication and a deeper bond. They'll be quicker to relax and seem more satisfied. It will have also increased your control in nearly all other situations, so why stop here?

All the tricks in this book can be taught to multiple species and many with the same training plans that you have here or, if you don't have any other pets, why not try using your imagination to see what other tricks you can come up with? We would love to see you capture these tricks and anything new you've decided to train on social media #teachmypet.

# Acknowledgements

Family has always been a big part of our lives and we would like to take this opportunity to thank our families. Both of us have lost our mums, so Santino, our son, doesn't have a grandmother. There is one lady who has taken on that role and who has become pivotal to our lives both personally and professionally. Christina, without you this book, the television series, in fact none of this would have been possible. We thank you from the bottom of our hearts. Chris, you're alright too.

David, Dad, you've inspired us to work hard and to provide our family with everything they need, just the way you did for your family.

There are about 1,000 people we would like to thank but our editor told us to keep this bit short. Jamie, said editor, thanks for your support. Karen, as always, we appreciate all the opportunities you have thrown our way.

We would like to thank our fantastic group of support trainers, including Dean Nicholas, Adrienne Critchlow, Bryony Neve, Veronika Spinkova, Lauren Watts, Alison Mercer, Emma Riedlinger and Kate Mallatratt. You were all picked because you're exceptional and you proved us right.

Romeo, Toby, Petucha, Minky, Balou, Zeus, Jack, Archie, Stanley, Rodney, Ella, Pablo, Fizz and Blake – the lessons that each of you taught us impact how we help and train other dogs every single day. Our love and passion for our work comes from our love for you.